ABOUT

Jay Davies used to w

and lives in Berkshire. She is married with

two daughters and three grandchildren.

Jay Davies

Walking Towards Light

Conversations that changed my life

Matador
9 Priory Business Park,
Wistow Road, Kibworth Beauchamp,
Leicestershire. LE8 0RX
Tel: (+44) 116 279 2299
Fax: (+44) 116 279 2277
Email: books@troubador.co.uk
Web: www.troubador.co.uk/matador

ISBN 978 1780883 083

British Library Cataloguing in Publication Data.
A catalogue record for this book is available from the British Library.

Typeset by Troubador Publishing Ltd, Leicester, UK

Matador is an imprint of Troubador Publishing Ltd

Printed and bound in the UK by TJ International, Padstow, Cornwall

MIX
Paper from
responsible sources
FSC
www.fsc.org
FSC® C013056

To those who talked and listened,
thank you for all the conversations we had together
which helped my understanding.

CONTENTS

INTRODUCTION

I hadn't really intended to write this book and yet friends had often said to me that it would be helpful to read some of the things I had talked about with them. So when I started working with Sebastian and he suggested the idea of writing, I decided I would look back at my life and try to make sense of all I had done and been. Maybe there would even be a book in there.

This book is not intended in any way to be definitive: it is the story of how I learned to look at life differently and expand my vision. I have imagined the reader face to face with me, as in my counselling days. We're all individuals and we live our lives at differing speeds and intensities, with our own priorities and beliefs. So I understand that your experiences may differ greatly from mine, and I just write from my own story.

I hope that somewhere among the pieces I have written you will find something which helps you, maybe opens up your mind and gives you a new perspective; perhaps even makes you consider making a change or a new choice. It may be just a few words that will resonate and stay in your mind afterwards. Or when you cannot accept what I say, I just ask you to see it as part of me.

While working on this book I went through a roller-coaster of emotions myself, as I learned new ideas and ways to be. I see this unsettling phase as normal and part of moving forward to something and somewhere better. And gradually I came through and started to reshape my life with new parameters. My scepticism faded and left me.

I am a different person now, and much more content and grounded. I hope you can take something from this book to help you feel the same.

SEBASTIAN

Have you ever had a person come into your life who seems to change your complete way of thinking and being, and open up all possibilities for you?

"Why don't you go and see Sebastian?" Fenella says suddenly one day. "I've been thinking about suggesting it for a while and feel it's the right time now." She's talked about him before, a friend of hers, who works as a Zen Shiatsu practitioner and is also a spiritual healer. Now I trust Fenella utterly, because she has counselled and supported me through many dark days. I am intrigued who this man is, as I've often heard her speak of him, and always with great affection and respect. She gives me his phone number. Next day I ring him and suddenly I am speaking to this Sebastian. He cheerily asks me to tell him a bit about me. He seems to know about me. We chat for some time and I remember warming to his energy and humour. I couldn't wait to meet him.

On paper he's a therapist who practises Shiatsu healing, a hands-on technique, aiming to harmonise the flow of energy through the meridians that run through the body. He works to clear blockages, which cause physical problems and potential illness, and in so doing moves energy through the body to heal and clear away stress and tension.

In his Shiatsu work he heals silently, drawing down energy from above and using his mind to receive guidance as to where the problems are and where to work in particular. Once I was lucky enough to watch him work on someone else, and saw with my own eyes how he was able to identify the source of pain in someone he had only just met, without being told what or where the problem was. I watched him work on her silently, drawing down energy to heal through his hands, and as he worked her pain level dropped. I cannot tell you what it was like to see and even feel this healing taking place before my very eyes. To be there in person, seeing someone's pain reduced and lifted by a true spiritual healer is a both exciting and slightly unnerving experience. I shall never forget it.

Sebastian knows me now as well as anyone does, and has become a key person in my life. We meet at regular intervals, and once we sit down and start to talk I forget where I am and am just in the moment, listening, writing, talking. There's no sense of time. He's lovely, funny, pertinent and challenging. We laugh a lot, but sometimes I find myself crying. We travel from the everyday to profound.

Right back in those early days, I saw that this was a place where I could trust and be listened to with acceptance and understanding. What I hadn't expected was that from the first meeting my fixed patterns of thinking and doing would be challenged. Actually, I like being challenged, and after all, I've come to Sebastian to find expansion, and feel ready for it.

At first I used to come home and rush in to write down from memory everything Sebastian had said that day. This habit came from the way I had trained as a marital counsellor, to listen, and write notes later. Fortunately this had helped me to develop a strong memory for what happened and what was said. But at the start of the fourth session Sebastian suddenly said, "Do you want to write things down now?" and I got out a pen and started to write down what was said, as much as I could manage, scribbling into a notebook.

The handwriting in my notebooks is proof of how fast I write, so the notes get transcribed the next day into something more organised and clear. Most of the stuff I write verbatim, the really important things I check as I go along, Sebastian often repeating them back to me, so I know I have understood. My ever growing notebooks are my guide and I refer to them constantly.

Sebastian told me at my very first session that I was a "very creative person", which led to me talking about my writing. I told him how I'd written poems for years and had been on a creative writing course, which I had loved, although I had found it highly demanding. Early on, we talked about the possibility of my writing about our meetings, especially how I might be able to share with others what I learned during them, and also from the experiences I've found special in my life. I've been lucky enough to have had many different challenges and I've always tried to meet life head on, embracing whatever happens with acceptance and courage.

For a long time I've seen my life choices and experiences as a ladder; each rung taking me forward, building on what I've just done or learned: teaching, counselling, youth justice work, writing. This ladder image grew in my head from my late teens and is still with me, hence the driving sense of purpose my life has always seemed to have. Meeting and working with Sebastian feels part of that ladder, and so, I feel, is writing this book. So this will be my book, and his of course, because I wouldn't be writing it without him. His energy, drawn down from above, heals my mind, body and soul, and opens up my thinking and doing. And my writing, as well.

LABELS

The day of my first meeting with Sebastian is a real eye-opener. I haven't met him until now and have only given him a brief outline of my situation when we arranged to meet. So now here we are, face to face for the first time. I launch into my story straight away; a familiar and well-worn story which I return a lot to in my head. I hear my voice trawling through my years of struggle, until he stops me. "You keep using negative words like 'terrible', 'daunting' and 'difficult' to describe what's happened in your life," he says.

I'm taken quite aback. This is not going to be a stroll in the park. Only a few minutes into our first meeting and he's challenging me already. "You see," he said, "you keep talking about the past being 'difficult', but the past is over. You're bringing words like bad and difficult into the present, by expecting it."

He went on to say that I was the one creating difficulty for myself. I had no idea what he could mean. He reminded me that I'd talked about a "difficult phone call", and how I dreaded ringing back the next time. "That's what happens if you come away from the call labelling it 'difficult'. The next time you go to pick up the phone or ring that person you will make it a difficult call. You'll be feeling anxious and the negativity will be passed on, and you will still hold most of the bad feeling inside yourself."

All these negative words, all this general negativity. Do I talk like that all the time and focus on the down side? Strange, because I'd always seen myself as strong and positive. He told me to listen to how I talked. I was appalled. Every few sentences I'd hear myself falling back and even when I saw a negative coming I found I couldn't replace it easily. "Not too bad" seemed the best I could do. This is my first meeting with Sebastian. What on earth will he think of me?

"You can correct negative statements. Just say to yourself: 'I cancel that statement.' Then say what you mean. Don't label things 'good' or 'bad'. Things just are. You're judging yourself critically how you were in the past, as well. Don't be so hard on yourself," he said at the end of our first meeting. I remember reeling home, thinking today had been challenging but I felt lighter. I didn't realise back then, of course, how much our meetings would change me.

I had a feeling that I would build a strong and

important relationship with Sebastian, and I had an intuitive feeling right from the start that I would learn from him in a very special way. I also recognised that I wanted to learn all he could tell me, and that in return I would devote as much time and energy as I could to putting it into practice.

I started thinking about what we'd talked about. What purpose do these labels serve?

This is what I realised:

❖ Labels define the nature of something. They are tags which help you to identify and differentiate.

❖ Labels are tags to allow you to recognise and understand what qualities belong to situations, objects or people, and therefore you can think or act accordingly. I know there are some 'dangerous' bends on a country road near my friend's house, so I am prepared for them and slow down when I get near.

❖ If you attach a label to someone, it could get fixed. If someone is labelled 'mean', you will expect them to be ungenerous and you may look for those qualities in them.

❖ And because labels set up expectations, if I say: "He's never going to change," that doesn't help him or me to change. I just expect him not to want to change. And I won't find it easy if he does.

And what did Sebastian mean about me creating the difficulty for myself? I think he means that if you label something bad, or good, and think about it enough, then you reinforce the thought sufficiently to make it happen. This then increases the likelihood of you actually acting on it. That's how you set up what will be bad or good for yourself and others.

Sebastian is always talking about how we get stuck in the unhelpful patterns we set and unwittingly fix for ourselves. It makes you think, doesn't it?

EXPECTATIONS

And then I found myself wondering about expectations. I remembered Sebastian had said to me at one point: "Don't have expectations of people. And just be aware that we often need to change what we look for in each other." He explained that loving someone unconditionally actually frees you from judgement and expectation. "Love others unconditionally without expectation, and do things for people without expectation of reward or thanks," said Sebastian.

Isn't expectation a joyful thing, about looking ahead and seeing happy events in the future that you want to anticipate happening? I certainly look forward to birthdays, the chance to celebrate, give and receive. We all welcome holidays for the chance to rest or do something we enjoy in different surroundings. But I suppose Sebastian was reminding me of the other side of expectations.

You've only got to think of Christmas and how the expectations around 'Make Christmas perfect for you and your family' have reached totally unrealistic and unnecessary proportions. It's the pressure to make things 'perfect' (a label to be avoided at all costs), that leads to anxiety, stress, and ultimately disappointment. When things don't work out the way you plan, then it's easy to become upset or cross at things not working out the way you'd hoped and expected.

The trouble is expectations can make our happiness dependent on our desires being fulfilled. That creates a cage for us, making our future happiness conditional on something often totally beyond our control. We can't control the future, and we don't see what's coming. "Stuff happens," as Sebastian would say.

And what about the expectations that are around you that you aren't even aware of? Inside yourself, your family, at work or school, within social groups and society itself. Expectations that are built into the systems that we live with on a daily basis. Expectations can start like seeds sown in our childhood, that grow and take on a life of their own. Expectations, like labels, get passed on down the line and become, 'what we do in our family.' Lots of family routines and behaviour patterns start that way, like in my family of teachers, who many generations ago set up expectations of high academic achievement. Patterns of relationships are unconsciously determined by what's deemed normal and expected 'in our family.' What's acceptable. It's not always easy to meet the expectations of others.

Expectations are also about wanting to be in control. I remember what happened to me when I went to see the Grand Canyon in Arizona, USA. I'd talked about going for years and it had been my lifelong dream to visit it, you know, the 'I must do this before I die' sort. So it was clearly to be the high spot and real highlight of our American holiday. The morning we're actually going, we wake very early in a hotel not many miles from the South Rim, and I'm not just excited, giggly and barely able to function, but also really scared. The nearer we get to it, the more panicked I remember feeling. I'll never forget what a shock it was to feel that. I was taken aback by the almost fear mounting inside me. What if it isn't as good as in the photos? What if we've picked a day when the view of the Canyon is obscured by low cloud? What if I'm disappointed? What will I do then, after all these years of looking at pictures of it, waiting and wanting to come, and now here I am and maybe it's not what I expected? I need the sun, to be blown away by the vast scale of it, an awesome sight to take my breath away. What if it's not as perfect as I really need it to be?

So what are expectations?

❖ Expectations are about the future and may be realistic or unrealistic.

❖ Expectations can lead to surprise, if the outcome is not in line with what is expected.

❖ Expectations can also cause disappointment, if not in line with what is expected.

❖ Expectations are a way to try and control the future and so feel safer about it. However, we can't control what happens in the next few minutes, never mind further ahead.

❖ In order to try and feel safer about what lies ahead, we set up expectations and then feel disconcerted or thrown into unwelcome anxiety if circumstances alter what we are expecting.

❖ Expectations can be our way of trying to control people as well as events. What we expect from others can be overtly asked for or just built into the way we live.

❖ Expectations focus on outcomes and results. If

we let go of trying to control these we will feel less burdened and more free.

❖ Expectations can actually make us fearful, because of the memory of a bad experience: a filling at the dentist, a driving lesson, a phone call we don't want to make.

Sebastian says: "Fear is false expectations appearing real. Things we fear often don't occur, but we get stuck, because we think they will, and that paralyses us."

ASKING QUESTIONS

The thing about Sebastian is he's always asking questions. He listens very carefully as I talk, and just when I think I'm doing fine he suddenly springs a question at me, like an arrow straight into the middle of my words, scattering them all over the floor. "Why don't you love yourself?" he asks. I sit, floored, unable to think or reply.

Actually I like being asked questions, because it allows me to work out what I do think and questions make me really reflect on what I do believe. I really like asking questions too, because questions are invitational, and often bring interesting answers which push you forward in your understanding of life. The best conversations are ones where you learn by being stretched and challenged. Questions do this, because they open up. Statements define and restrict. Questions invite an answer, and don't end in a full stop.

And Sebastian's questions always take me far, opening up new and deeper areas for me to reflect on. I like being challenged. "You find out what's going on when you ask questions, and then you can walk accordingly," he says.

I find that certain questions stop me in my tracks. Sebastian's fond of these, and I never see them coming. Some time ago I was talking to him about the way I take things to heart in an argument, and find them hard to put aside, an old pattern going back to childhood. I remember I paused, and then the unexpected arrow came: "And does it serve you well?"

"Ask when you do things: 'Does it serve me?', and if it doesn't, choose to change it," he said. "Of course if you want to carry on as you've always done, that's up to you. It's your choice." He sounded brisk.

I was complaining the other day that I was a bit fed up that I hadn't been helped the way I needed. It's far too easy to blame, I know. Sebastian went straight to the point: "Instead of what you need from him, what is missing from you?"

I write the question down.

How are you with asking yourself questions?

HABITS

I was reading recently an article in an educational supplement that talked about how a new 'no excuses' policy is being implemented in some inner-city schools to deal with the high level of bad behaviour and unacceptable rule breaking. The school featured had set up a new scheme made up of just five clear simple rules which the pupils had to obey if they were not to get detentions. These involved uniform, classroom behaviour, punctuality, bringing the right equipment to school, and homework to be done adequately and on time. Pupils could expect a same-day detention for even the smallest infringement, and no exceptions were made.

The bit that was interesting was that when the scheme had settled in, everyone, the children, teachers and parents felt calmer. They all knew what to expect and what was expected of them, and understood that these rules were there to create a better atmosphere in which to work, concentrate and achieve. When this was coupled with positive incentives, pupils saw it was better for them to behave. The school became a happier place to learn and work and be.

Schools, like individuals, develop systems or habits without realising how they are becoming endemic, and then need to change them. It's easy to build up habits, and we don't realise how past experiences programme our minds into how we expect the present to be. It's very easy to just say: "That's how it is in our family / school, and that's what we do".

Habits make life easier, because you don't have to think as much. You turn to the safety of familiar routines which don't require a lot of thought, and habit allows you not to have to make choices as much. It allows you to stay where you are. Change can be scary too and if you try to change a bad habit it's all too easy to stop and revert to how it was before. Back to the familiar. Perhaps there's a pay-off in staying as you are?

I hadn't realised how stuck I was until Sebastian and I were talking about my resistance to change. I confess I've had a long problem with apologising and forgiving, born out of my parents' insistence that I say I was sorry. I'd be sent upstairs to my bedroom until I did. I was prepared to stay up there forever, just so long as I didn't have to apologise for something I felt I hadn't said or done. I couldn't forgive them either.

19

Injustice is a powerful force. I knew this feeling still persisted in me, and had left a legacy of resistance.

"It takes a long time for you to forgive," Sebastian said. "This has served you in the past, but it doesn't any longer." Bad habits often get stuck early on, because as children when we feel upset and misunderstood we feel alone and so set up behaviour patterns to help us be noticed and heard. The same as the badly behaving pupils in school. When they can't cope with the work or academic demands on them, they create mayhem.

Habits, bad or good, can work for us in getting the response or result we require, but they can easily become a sort of default position which we later rely on, just because they're old patterns which feel familiar. Sebastian told me that, now I recognised forgiving as a problem, it gave me a choice. "You need to decide if you want to carry on this way, or if you stay in the same place, that it's your choice." It feels quite a shock to be told by someone else that you're *choosing* to stay stuck in a bad habit.

I could see what he meant though, because once you realise something, you needn't be stuck any more. It frees you to change something, although any sort of habits can take time and effort to shift. They can lead to inertia, rather than active change. "Habits are what make you what you are," he said, "but people normally think 'I am who I am, and who I've always been.'"

So here is my favourite advice from Sebastian: "Ask when you do things: does it serve me well?"

FEAR

Fear can be fun: adrenalin, excitement, pushing yourself to new heights, taking risks. But fear can also be anything but fun when it starts to get in the way of living life the way you want to. Anxiety can so easily build from childhood into blocks which interfere with our minds and limit our range of possibilities.

In the past I tried to meet my own fears as a challenge, and I saw fear as a driver towards achievement, although it did cost me in terms of stress. I used to try to power through anxiety, knowing that if I recognised what I was afraid of, looked it in the eye and did it anyway, I would be rewarded by knowing I had not given in. One of my problems was a fear of being out of control, a common fear. Lots of people suffer with this, because when you feel weighed down with responsibility, at times you can feel overwhelmed. You can find yourself thinking endlessly about the situation that lies ahead that scares you. What if? What will I do then? Fear is an exhausting business.

You can churn through imagined scenarios and

potential outcomes and weigh up in advance where the anxiety lies, so you'll be ready to deal with it. I used to call it 'mine sweeping': looking at situations ahead, in order to anticipate how they will turn out and work out how you will behave and cope. It's a crazy and futile way of trying to be in control, since we can have no idea what will happen. I don't believe it does or can control fear either.

"How do you deal with fear?" I asked Sebastian. He knew that my need to help people had cost me hugely, taking on sometimes too much. He also knew the physical cost of this stress to me. I didn't often say no, even when I felt it was beyond me. He surprised me with his answer: "It's not fear itself that you're dealing with. It's the fear you have inside you. Fear is false expectations appearing real. Things that we fear often don't occur, but we get stuck, because we think they will and that paralyses us. You, your mind, created the fear, so your mind can take you away from it."

"But my fear's huge," I said. "No, it isn't," he replied. "The fear is smaller than you think. Think of a telescope. Turn the telescope round and look through it now. See the fear looking small." He reminded me of the link between mind and body, how the mind affects the body, and the body affects the mind.

"Overwrite the fear," he said. "Don't block it. If

you block it, it's still there. Think of something positive you can say to yourself when you feel fear, the opposite of what you're afraid of. Think of something that will give you strength. Be flexible though and change the words if another situation or fear crops up, which it will." He gives me an example, a trip out, with me imagining and enjoying the feeling of being there already. "Say 'I'm doing this. It's good. I'm already there.' In your mind, go straight to where you want to be. Miss out all the bit in the middle," he says.

"Straighten up, have happy thoughts in your head. Sing a happy song. Your body says everything's great. Energy comes down from your mind into your body and frees you up. That's the way to get rid of fear," he says.

He often comes back to the problem of fear and anxiety and has given me ways to alleviate it:

❖ If you're troubled by something, take that and imagine it positively.

❖ If you can't sleep for worrying about the next day, before you go to bed take 15 minutes and write down your thoughts about the coming day, how it will work out.

❖ If there's something you're afraid of, say spiders, keep imagining a scenario where spiders are pleasant and you're handling them happily.

❖ Don't at any time think of the original experience which started the unhelpful thoughts in the first place i.e. the past.

❖ Don't anticipate anything bad happening in the future either. The unhelpful thoughts will dissipate on their own, because you haven't let them into your imagination.

❖ If you're fearful, get out of the place of fear. Don't worry why you're in it.

LOVING YOURSELF

"Why don't you love yourself?" was one of the first things I remember Sebastian saying to me. This completely floored me. 'Love yourself'? What a strange concept. Surely loving is about other people. And anyway, despite a loving, stable childhood, it wasn't really part of our family way to focus on yourself. I think the lack of parental siblings, with no aunts, uncles or cousins, meant that we looked inwards and were a tight foursome. I grew up feeling I was just one quarter of the family, and therefore only relevant as the fourth and youngest in the hierarchy. We were taught to look out for others, and when the day was over you just went to bed and hoped to do the same tomorrow.

But Sebastian's question unsettled me and lingered in my mind after I got home. He often came back to it in our conversations, and I would find us back talking about my attitude to myself. I knew I hadn't bothered to look after myself as any sort of priority, especially consider any demands on my health and stress. The trouble was I was driven in my counselling years by my ever present sense of responsibility. I felt a bit like Atlas holding up the world. My husband, family, children and home all needed me, as well as clients and counsellors, especially those in training. But you can't make demands on your body, year in, year out, without being in danger of getting overwhelmed. I think I knew I was heading for disaster, that if anything big happened in my personal life I had no space to deal with it.

Then my mother died suddenly, a total and devastating shock. A close friend moved away. One of my daughters decided to go and live in Australia. My mind said: "Carry on, you can cope." My broken heart didn't agree, but I kept going anyway. Then a serious chest infection which wouldn't go away and turned into hepatitis. Not an illness you can ignore, and one I should have taken seriously. Except I didn't. If you don't allow yourself to rest and recover from an illness like that properly, and you don't draw energy into yourself in any way, you're setting up serious problems for the future.

There's only so much your body can take before it rebels and gives in again. Hepatitis, then back to work too soon and ten more years of illness, injuries and deaths in the family. Even the dog became paralysed. Heavy years: new work challenges, new grandchildren too far away in Australia. Stress and loss coloured our lives. And then it happened again. Total burn out.

This time it took four years for my mind, body and soul to recover. I slept and cried. I rested and read spiritual books. For the first time in my life I focused on me and me alone. Actually, I had no other choice. I felt empty, my identity and energy all gone. I felt nothing and nobody. It was a huge feeling that strangely enough seemed to be acceptable, because there was nothing I could do to change it. When the whole world stops you accept help and are just grateful to be looked after. And be loved.

I was drawn to reading endlessly about mind, body and soul, but mostly soul. It filled the hole inside me and restored my spirit. As I built up more strength I turned to gentle pursuits. I taught myself to paint, gardened and started to write again. I made a space just for me, a space which changed me forever and which I now regard as a miracle. It led me to working with Sebastian, who has transformed my life.

I remember him telling me that my body had worked so hard to keep me alive that I should thank it every day for bringing me back to health again: "You'll never be able to pay off the debt. Love your body, be joyful, read spiritual books, take exercise." Then he said something very strange. "Apologise to your body, then say thank you for the past, right up to the present.

Say thank you for how it's going to support you in the future. Promise your body that you'll walk down the path together. Before, your mind dragged your body into it." He's right about that, and I do want to change, but where do I start?

I went back to the books where I had written down what Sebastian had told me. I made a list from them that would show me the path:

How to love myself:

❖ Just be and be joyful. Be where I am and accept how it is.

❖ Always be good to myself, and make sure I look after myself. Don't push myself.

❖ Give myself the gift of time and allow time in my schedule to be peaceful. Meditate more, it helps relaxation.

❖ Live in the moment and live for today.

❖ Be peaceful. Watch the world go by. This makes me stop and be present more of the time.

❖ Put myself at the top of the ladder. That gives me the ability to look after other people. If I need to have a reason to put myself first, I should think what might happen if I don't.

❖ Smile at everything, including myself. Choose fun and enjoyment.

❖ Learn to praise myself, not criticise. Don't be hard on myself, or beat myself up.

❖ Forgive myself quickly.

❖ Be OK with the pressure off. People often push themselves to look after others, instead of looking after themselves. If I want to help other people, I should match the way I do it to what I need.

❖ Keep looking after my health and well-being. Sleep well. Pace myself.

Things to say to myself:

❖ I am being kind to myself. I am at peace.

❖ I choose to be happy and stay in a place of unconditional love.

❖ I forgive myself easily. I don't have to say what for.

❖ I am blessed and I feel it.

I realised that I used to confuse being important to myself with 'self-importance', which is quite different, and is about ego and having an artificially high opinion of yourself. Loving yourself makes you feel more stable, because you know and like yourself better. You feel protected and more peaceful. Sebastian says: "If you love you, it fulfils a lot of your requirements, because it allows you to love others. Also you don't expect anything from other people."

ALL THE REASONS

I would love myself, except
the mirror says 'You're no-one special.'
You've got to trust a mirror.
The mirror is saying:
'You're a six out of ten person,
and don't you forget it.'

I would love myself, except
there are better people,
much better to put first.
You see, the people that deserve it
most, those you put first.
How could it be otherwise?

I would love myself, except
I wouldn't elevate myself
to so lofty a place.
But my heart listened:
"One day you will be different.
Your time will come."

And now I love myself, except
to live in worth and joy,
that is a gift from God.

LOVING OTHERS

❖ Loving others can be the greatest joy we have.

❖ Love unconditionally, without expecting return. It's up to others what they do with it.

❖ Tell those you love that you love them, every day.

❖ Unconditional love is saying "I don't need anything from you".

❖ If you're seeing love, compassion and joy in someone else, those things are in you too.

❖ Love others without expectation.

❖ When you love, see the person the best they can be, not the worst.

❖ Enjoy the loves that run through your life and

make a point of telling those people that you love them.

❖ Love others and give them the freedom to decide how or when they want to change or go forward.

❖ Love like you've never been hurt.

TRUSTING YOURSELF

I suppose most of us are fortunate enough to have someone to trust, a partner, family, friends; people we can rely on to stand by us when the chips are down. But, when something big happens to you, maybe something unexpected and distressing, you can find yourself disorientated and the normal parameters of what you know changed. It's then that you lose trust in who you are.

It's then you can't find the person inside you that you were, because somebody else has taken their place. This may be temporary or permanent. I remember when I had hepatitis I felt I'd gone away somewhere, but wasn't sure where. I'd lost my spark and my energy, and with that my desire to do anything at all. Who was this strange person lying in bed, not even wanting to lift a book? It feels very frightening to lose yourself.

I lost myself literally the day I had a bad accident. I tripped over a doorstep and pitched forward, hitting my forehead and nose full on, on the back of an oak dining chair. To lose my face to a bruised and swollen mess was a devastating shock, and I felt like an alien, hardly recognising myself in the mirror. It took weeks to feel able to leave the house and go out. But the hardest thing of all was the loss of trust in myself. If I have fallen once I can fall again. Even benign places and situations seemed to pose a potential danger as I struggled, fighting this new vulnerability. It coloured everything I did.

I went to Sebastian to ask for help. "Is God a part of you?" he asked. "Do you trust in him?" I said I did. "Then do you trust you?" I didn't need to answer. "Keep telling yourself that you have confidence and be content. Accept yourself where you are, it's then easier to move forward."

Sebastian's words, like beacons, encourage and lead me out of darkness to a safer place.

LOST

I stopped counting the months
that muffled autumn, a muted falling,
weakening sunshine, early mists
nudging out a dying summer with
tongues of orange flame I did not see.

This was the year I saw in monochrome,
lay distant, gone away; fatigue like deadened
glass holding me in, stopping me breathe, till
standing at my bedside they watched me vanish,
cross into emptiness and hollow sleep.

Woke to stopped clocks, lengthening days,
skeletons of beech and sycamore filling for spring,
taut shapes against a bright landscape,
colours edging forward, crisp and sharp,
the freshness of green.

LEAVING THE PAST BEHIND

Sebastian was always telling me in the beginning that I was carrying too much inside me from the past, and that the weight of what I had carried for other people through my work was still with me. I knew that the reason I had become ill was that I was still carrying grief and trauma inside me. And it had been building up for years. I think I'd thought that time would just heal the feeling. Now two years later, I saw that I had to find energy and joy again.

People often get stuck when they're unhappy. They feel depressed and don't know how to shake off misery. Friends and family can come up with all kinds of suggestions, but pain is a very personal thing. For some, the answer is counselling, for others it's being positive and just soldiering on, long walks, going to the GP for tablets, talking to friends, anything that suits you. But however you do it, you need to let go of the pain, because pain can really affect your state of mind and well-being. The more you hold it all inside, the more overwhelmed you become, like I did.

Sebastian explained that we carry the past: pain, experiences and memories, on our backs, like rocks in a rucksack. The rucksack weighs us down and slows us up, getting in the way of our happiness. Happiness is about feeling light and free. We need to put the weight down and not carry and refill the rucksack all the time. "All the rocks you were carrying in your rucksack were from the past," he said, "and you're still carrying them around. No wonder you feel so burdened sometimes." He told me to get rid of the past, and I would be lighter.

Then he told me how. He said I could imagine a place and take the rucksack down off my back and leave it in that imaginary place. In my mind I chose a big oak tree, a tree that I had recently sat under. "Now, put the rucksack down under the tree," he said. "It will always be there under the tree you are imagining, and because the rucksack contains your past, you may sometimes want to go back to it and look at part of it. The past can be like a book you read. Open the rucksack, take the book out, read it, and you will now be detached from it. That way you don't connect your heart to it, so you'll be able to read without all the emotions."

How amazing to be able to *choose* to walk away from the past I no longer need to carry. I can revisit the parts I want when I like, but I don't need to hang on to the painful bits. My past then becomes just my story. I'm learning that the past is gone and you can't go back and change it. Leave it, and live as much as you can in the now. Be aware how much you will change for yourself if you do. You'll feel lighter and more joyful, and you will have more space for energy and creativity.

I was left feeling elated at the thought of getting away from all that gloom and weight. However, several things still bothered me:

❖ I had lost so many years of good health and well-being by not understanding how bad it is to hold on to trauma and pain. However I suddenly realised that even having that thought was exactly what I shouldn't be doing so many years on: worrying about the lost years which I can do nothing about.

❖ I had allowed myself to not look after myself, believing that my duty was to be there first and foremost for others.

❖ I had been expecting life to be difficult for me, and I got what I expected. But I've just learned I don't need expectations, nor to have a difficult life any more.

❖ I could see that there had been a curious comfort in dwelling on the 'difficult' past and thinking about it so much. I realised it had been a kind of 'proof' to me that I had faced all kinds of awful situations, and had weathered the storm. But I now see that my new belief in myself will be much more effective.

❖ So, if the past now stays in the past, I have to start living more in the now. I don't need to rely on the past to guide me, but can trust in myself as I become more aware of things that work for me.

❖ I could also see that I had demanded too much of my body and caused it stress. I could change that now by letting go of a need to control so much. I can be more open to letting things just happen.

Sebastian said to me early on: "You'll be much lighter if you put down the weight of all this stuff inside you, this grief and trauma. Just do it. And you like writing. You could write about it too."

I was also lucky to have a friend who opened

another door for me, who taught me that painting can be anything you want it to be: a way to escape, exciting, comforting, or just fun. At school I'd been led to believe I was no good at art. But she showed me that all you need is a blank piece of paper, pencil, brushes, paints, and you can create any colour, any picture, anything you want. It can help you be free.

WATERCOLOUR

Ashes Hollow, steep, lonely valley,
rocky outcrops forcing their way
through prickly grass where sheep,
stamping their feet as we approach
call to their lambs, demanding,
and the clear stream tumbles, bubbles icy down
to Little Stretton, the sun fitful on our backs.

She's holding the blues and whites in her head,
remembering the lime of the tree halfway up the hill,
the shades of sage and olive as the clouds pass over
and the deep textures soften, till the colours are taken
out of her mind, mixed with water and allowed
to trickle down the paper, the water glistening
as the brush starts to move.

She climbs into the picture, and it's as if there
has never been the darkness of those months,
as if all the hopelessness is flowing away down
the hills, the brush sweeping aside the black,
releasing the ochre and green, and there is
no time, only watercolour in the peace
and she stays in the painting and is safe.

GRATITUDE

A long time ago a good friend gave me a pretty little Indian notebook with a beautiful pale orange silk cover, embroidered with red, gold and white edged flowers. It had lined pages and a thin satin bookmark, trailing lovely glass beads of pale yellow and black. I kept it for ages, hoping one day I'd find a special reason to write in it.

"Have you got a little book you could write in?" Sebastian said. "I think it would be good for you to write a 'gratitude diary'. You're now standing up for yourself and making new boundaries. Be where you are and how it is. And now start to write down all the good things in your life. It helps to raise your frequency."

I didn't understand what a gratitude diary was, and I knew even less about 'raising my frequency', but at least I knew what book I could use. "To start with, in the morning write down twenty things you're grateful for, and write them down for ten days only. After that, write down your gratitude for twenty things in the morning, and twenty different things in the evening, but this time for thirty days. After that you can choose," he said.

Think about it. The task is to write down in your little book every morning for ten days twenty things you are grateful for. Now I've always seen myself as a fairly grateful person, brought up to say 'please' and 'thank you' at all appropriate times. We even, as I recall, as children wrote 'thank you' letters on *Christmas Day* in the afternoon, before we even got to the Christmas cake. So you'd think I'd be up for twenty things, daily. At first I felt a bit panicky. Would I think of different things every day? Were you 'allowed' to repeat yourself if you got 'stuck'?

As luck would have it the next day happened to be the first of the month, so that felt auspicious. Every morning I sat and wrote when I got up or after breakfast. After ten days of thinking I was doing really well I decided to read what I'd written, only to find I'd not written twenty a day at all, only ten. I've always read instructions in a rushed way. And now I have to write *twenty* in the morning and *another twenty* in the evening for *thirty days.*

I suppose you could call it 'counting your blessings'. I would sit and look out of the window and see so much to be grateful for. Healthy people walking down the road. Children going to school. Birds, trees, flowers, roads, cars. Loving husband, daughters, family, friends, neighbours. Food in the cupboard, turn on the tap: clean water to drink, hot water in the shower. Central heating when it gets cold. Books to read and knowing how to read and write, moments of sheer happiness...and I did my '40 for 30 days', no problem. And I loved it.

What I didn't realise was that by writing the diary I would feel different. You see, the more I wrote it, the more I felt and noticed things to be grateful for. I also started to feel a more positive person. You see the world in a new light. I felt uplifted by appreciating and enjoying the world around me: that is, I 'raised my frequency'. Sebastian says that the more gratitude you are aware of and actually feel, the more you attract positive energy into your life and the more positive a person you become. Good for you and others.

I felt happier and more aware of what is important and what is not. I thought over what Sebastian had told me about gratitude:

❖ Gratitude helps by lifting you and allowing you to feel better.

❖ Gratitude also allows you to accept and love people as they are.

❖ But it does other things too. Sebastian told me that I could stop being angry or upset with someone by using gratitude. "When you get upset with someone, stop and think of ten things that make you grateful for them," he said. "It will send any bad feeling of yours away. Gratitude does that."

❖ He's always telling me that we need to remember we are part of nature and must care for and love our environment. We should also be respectful of everything, however small. "Be grateful for everything, including the ant walking across the path. Everything matters."

❖ Sebastian surprised me one day by saying: "If you're in a grateful frame of mind you can be grateful for the things you like in yourself and also the things you dislike." I recall asking: "Why would I want to like the bad bits of me?" The answer came: "Because they are part of you. You can't be in a place of gratitude and a place of dislike at the same time. So if you are in a place of gratitude and start to think what you dislike about yourself, you do start to like it." He went on to say that if we love and accept ourselves, good and bad alike, then it makes it easier for us to change things.

❖ Watch out in case a debt of gratitude traps you. If you feel you owe someone something, it's hard not to feel controlled by that feeling. If someone is very kind to you and you feel indebted, then you can get stuck by either feeling dependent on them, or not being able to free yourself emotionally from them. "Be OK with yourself, be where you are and accept how it is. Dismiss the idea of a 'debt' to them."

❖ Gratitude works a bit like a circle. The more you're grateful, the more gratitude and blessings you feel, and will receive. Whatever you focus on you bring towards you.

It's funny how you can get thank you letters and you're very pleased, but others really touch your heart. I keep a brown envelope which contains all my 'special' letters. Occasionally I get them out and read them. Gary's was one of them. Actually it was a Christmas card.

I met Gary when I decided to become a volunteer One-to-One literacy tutor in a Young Offenders

Institution. My job was to help with reading and writing with young lads of about 14-18 years, some of whom couldn't even write their own name or address. Gary was in for about 6 months, as I remember, so we worked together for quite a while.

Every Wednesday morning he would be unlocked from his cell and we'd go to a classroom, often on the same wing, just the two of us, Gary and me. The agenda generally depended on what help the boys needed and asked for: 'help with theory for the bricks course', 'write letters to sister' or 'improve spelling'. Imagine too, what it's like to be away from home for the first time in your life and have to have your mother's or girlfriend's letter read to you, and not be able to reply.

The lads, by and large, liked one-to-one. Boredom is rife in a prison and one-to-one means you have something to do, and get out of your cell for an hour or two. If it's your first experience of prison you can feel a bit lost on a wing of sixty inmates. So someone who comes into the prison just for you and brings you pictures and stories of things you like, as well as simple word games and puzzles, now that's special. "Are you coming again next week, Miss?" they would ask.

Gary's aim was to improve his handwriting and 'write better letters home'. I loved the relationship we built together week on week, the often tiny progress we would make together, the fun we had. Gary had spent some weeks working in a garage, he said, and he'd talk endlessly about body sprays and how to strip down an engine. I'd make up worksheets about the garage and he'd fill in the answers with joined-up writing. He wanted to work in a garage when he got out.

Gary left after some months, one Christmas. I've still got the Christmas card he gave me. It's of a snowman with a red and yellow striped hat and scarf, surrounded by mice and rabbits. Such an unlikely card from a sixteen year old boy, but such a touching surprise, and more to the point, hand-written in joined-up writing:

"Thank you for every think you have done for me and coming to see me every time it has bean very good Betwene us two it has gone so well and it is going to be very sad leaving you after all them seshons we had."

That year it was my best Christmas card. You don't expect thanks from a sixteen year old in prison.

CHOICES

Some years ago I found myself too exhausted and unable to go out much, and when I felt better I just wanted to go where I felt safe and where people accepted me as I was. Spending a lot of time at home made me look inwards, which is what you need to do to recover, however it makes you forget about the external pressures of normal living. One of the things I found hardest was the returning demand of making choices. When you're ill or bereaved you lean on others to make decisions and choices for you, and it was a shock to come out of what felt like hibernation to take over making my own choices again.

I remember a new feeling that my whole sense of priorities had changed. I didn't like shopping anymore, because there were far too many choices to make. Choices can be overwhelming. I found myself in the supermarket stressed by all the different makes of any one item, specific labelling on fat, salt, sugar content, current offers: 3 for 2s, buy one get one free, not to mention voucher and coupon use.

I didn't want to be bothered with what to wear and every morning I was tempted to put on the same as I'd worn yesterday, because opening the wardrobe doors faced me with too much choice. Particularly when we had to go out somewhere special, I'd stand in the bedroom panicked and paralysed by the potential combinations of colour and suitability, literally unable to make a choice.

"What do you want for dinner tonight?" the daily question. "Do you want fish or chicken or something with pasta?" The same problem, the same response. "You choose. You know what I like," I'd say. I felt lucky to have someone willing to tolerate my frequent indecision and be prepared to decide for me. But you can't go on like that for ever and you can't run away from choosing for yourself.

Sebastian said to me one day: "Choices make you powerful, and responsible too, because you are saying 'I actively make a choice for it.'" And of course, that was the whole point. I couldn't at that stage cope with responsibility, and choice brings responsibility with it.

It's a common feature of institutions that within them you are limited in your choices. If you've ever been in hospital you'll no doubt have experienced restrictions on what you're allowed to do, when you can get out of bed, walk about, eat or drink, see visitors, go home. And when you do it can feel very strange, to be back to all the constant decision making, all the daily complications of the normal world.

I'll never forget what Ryan said to me, one of the lads I was helping in the Young Offenders Institution: "I quite like it in here, you know. You get meals to eat with your mates, you can listen to music, smoke and play pool. You get told what to do. You don't have to think." When you've been thrown out of school, and perhaps home as well, choices are limited. Often not being able to write or read adequately for employment, boredom and broken relationships, all lead to low self-esteem, and often alcohol and drug problems and crime... and custody.

UNDERSTANDING CHOICES

I can't believe the number of times Sebastian has used the word 'choices' to me. It's a word that governs my life now, and is the driver for how and where I want to be. You'll be thinking perhaps that that sounds selfish, but I'll need to explain.

If I go back to the beginning when Sebastian and I started to meet I was still in my 'haven't I been through a lot?' phase. He was sitting, listening, and I had thrown myself into an account of a recent episode when I'd been irritable and bad-tempered, justifiably in my view. "Well, that was your choice to be angry," he said calmly. I remember feeling very put out. He clearly hadn't understood what I was saying, otherwise he would have seen I had the right to be annoyed. I would have to tell him more of the detail until he realised what I went through. Old patterns die hard.

But you can't shift Sebastian. "We all make choices every moment of every day," he says. "We can choose to be annoyed or not, or choose to stay that way or not. We can choose to be in a place of unconditional love, or not."

I'm not sure I'd ever seen before that having an argument is a *choice*. Arguments are what just happen, because of – well, things. And is he saying I can make a choice to avoid an argument, and that it's another choice to carry on feeling aggrieved afterwards? This would be a radical change to embrace this concept. And even more so to put it into practice. "Don't blame others for your irritation. You choose to be irritated." The words ring in my ears on my way home.

He had already shown me that choices make you responsible and that when you say, "I choose" you're saying "I'm in control and can make my life what I want it to be." He went on to warn that if you don't believe you have choices, you then want to take choices away from other people. But as soon as you are aware and know your power to choose, you allow other people to live their lives, and realise you aren't responsible for the choices they make. That lifts the pressure on all sides and everyone feels better.

I certainly remember the difference I felt when I finally started to make choices for myself and stopped shouldering the weight of carrying choices for others in the family. And of course, the family didn't fall apart. Everyone seemed much freer and happier, especially me. I saw choices around me that I'd never seen before, and felt more willing to make them. I told

Sebastian I was glad to have an opportunity to test new things out. "Those opportunities were always there. You just didn't see them. Now you can see them, you're able to make choices. They're not done to you."

He went on: "All this means you have power back in your hands and you choose how you want your life to be."

MANAGING CHOICES

How do you make choices? When I look back at the choices I've made over many years I find myself slightly horrified at how quickly the biggest and most important decisions got made. Quite disproportionate to the amount of money to be spent or the commitment involved. Marriage, buying houses, the children's names, choosing a dog: they all just sort of happened, and then were there. Maybe that's one way to deal with the responsibility of making such a big choice, and the right one too. It feels right, so let's do it. Quick, before logic sets in and we start a list of pros and cons and get totally bogged down.

My childhood family was a mini-democracy, very mini, being just the four of us. Our favourite pastime was to sit at the kitchen table and just move seamlessly from breakfast to coffee, even sometimes to lunch, debating, laughing and discussing anything and everything, our very best sort of morning. 'What shall we do today?' would often be the topic, but by then either the morning was over or it was too late to go anywhere. We wouldn't all agree of course, in which case any family decision, even what TV programme to watch, would require a ballot. Each person would state their preference, paper would be given out and pencils allocated and each person would vote for one of the four choices. The trouble was, when number two, say, got the majority vote we would all decide we'd actually prefer one of the other numbers. We'd argue a bit and then the ballot was declared void. Choosing can be fun, but choices can be tricky.

They can also be seen as 'good' or 'bad', a scary responsibility. What if I make a *bad* choice? What will I do then? How many good /bad choices have I made in my life? And heavens, how on earth do you assess them? Surely each choice can bring both good and bad experiences. A skiing holiday could mean fantastic snow and fun, but you might break your leg. The hotel might have wonderful food, but the disappointing view is not how it looked online. Where does that leave you in the 'right/wrong choice' stakes?

You buy a lottery ticket on Jackpot day. You choose your numbers and you don't win. Bad choice. Or you do. Good choice? I wouldn't know, but we've all seen media pictures of new multi-millionaires smiling with the Big Cheque. We've also heard many stories of winners destroyed by the responsibilities of choice, how to spend/share/invest/give away- and how much.

I do know that I made and make my biggest decisions and choices very much by what feels right for me. I went into counselling, because something inside me said that this was a good choice and belonged to what I needed to learn and experience.

Sebastian told me one day to say: "I choose to be happy and stay in a place of unconditional love."

He added: "Say 'At all times I choose and know that I am blessed.'"

CIRCLES

It's really easy to get tired and not realise that you may be starting to go round a circle, which makes you behave in unhelpful ways. It starts when you're perhaps feeling driven to get something finished, or just deeply involved doing something you love, and you get caught up in pressure, possibly self-imposed. Or it may be pressure from outside: work, children, family, duties, and all you can see are the relentless demands and all you can feel is the tiredness. In my case it's often to do with some project I'm working on, and I'm so involved in it that I just can't stop. I stop being sensible and don't look after myself. I remember when I was writing booklets for use with Young Offenders I was at my worst in this respect. I just went on and on, especially at home on my own.

At one meeting with Sebastian I was telling him how annoyed I was that no-one had asked me how I was. I'd not slept well and felt I'd given my all to the family and no-one had noticed. "You feel bugged by things if you're tired," he said. "Tiredness is insidious.

It's like a vine that keeps on creeping. You don't notice it at first. It's like being dehydrated." He told me that when you're tired you have less self-respect and less respect for others and you have more arguments.

You stop looking after yourself and loving yourself and then you need love from outside you. That leads to expectations. If people don't give you what you need, (and you aren't even conscious that you need something, so how could they know?) you can get annoyed or depressed. It's a circle you can keep going round: tired, needing concern and love from others because you've forgotten to look after and love yourself. Expecting them to know what you want (without even telling them), feeling let down, cross, miserable, even more tired. I often felt quite stuck at this point.

However, you do have the power to alter circles if you wish. If you've forgotten to love yourself and others too maybe, choose to love again. If you've started to make demands on other people, stop expecting people to be where you are and know what you need. Only you know that. Be more peaceful with yourself and seek stillness. "If you treat yourself well, you'll treat others well," says Sebastian.

Sometimes circles provide a defence to contain fears we have in our intimate partnerships. It can be scary to be in an intimate relationship if you feel stifled by the closeness. Some people fear they are losing themselves, or maybe feel damaged within a powerful relationship, or are afraid they will be abandoned. To deal with these fears they unconsciously create a circle of conflict. Rows alienate, but also buy space, so in a curious way they may help, albeit only for a while.

The trouble is, when you have been alienated too long you can feel anxious and need to make up and be close again. Humans need togetherness, so they seek intimacy. But after a while it can feel too much again and lead to the old unconscious fears and anxiety coming back. So you provoke a row, and the circle starts again.

Do circles feature in your life? And if so, do they serve you well?

LISTENING

My work as a marital and relationship counsellor was where I was most at home. I loved sitting with men and women of all ages, with all the diverse problems they brought, helping them to make sense of where they were and how they had got there. I spent hundreds of hours, fifteen years in fact, working one to one or with couple partnerships. I trained with Relate and went on to supervise for them, later setting up a partnership counselling practice with a colleague.

If you want to learn about humanity, sitting with other people in a confidential setting allows you to get very close. It's where people tell you how it really is, their fears, what they find hard to talk about or have never dared to say before. I loved the changes they were able to make, the risks they took with my help, the peace and relief they found in taking control of a seemingly insoluble situation. It was good too to see counsellors coming through training and becoming gentle and loving with clients, able to use all the skills they had learned.

People come to Relate usually when they can't manage some element of communication. They are going through a crisis or dilemma that they may not be able to talk about, or even face inside themselves. Or they may have told all the people they know the ins and outs of their situation, about their despair or anger. They may have asked them for help and advice, which hasn't worked for them. More often they come for counselling because a partner isn't listening, or is too angry, fearful or sad to hear, and talking to each other becomes impossible.

Listening is actually quite a tricky business. The art of listening depends on many things: our current state of mind, our desire to hear what we need to, our desired intention. We may interrupt to contradict or steer the conversation the way we want. We may stop listening and drift off into thinking about our reply. We may stop listening, because we're anxious or impatient to know where the conversation is leading. That stops us hearing what's really being said, and then we wonder why we can't remember it afterwards. Chances are we'll remember the bits we wanted to hear and which fitted in with our own agenda. Memory can be very selective.

Interrupting is a major technique for sabotage. The speaker is stopped in mid-flow to be faced with shouting, denial or an alternative version. People who have problems with emotions tend to run, sometimes literally, from conversations that end in conflict or distress. Justifying gets in the way of listening too, when you sit there listening, desperate to say why you did it, the reason for it, how it was the best thing anyway. Often one's own view really does feel more valid.

When you've been together a long time, listening takes on an added dimension, because you have such a long shared history. Sometimes you listen and switch off, because you 'know' what he or she is going to say: the 'I've heard it all before' scenario. You think you know your partner so well that there's not much point in expecting anything new or interesting to be said. Don't waste your breath, I can read your mind. That doesn't leave much expectation of, or room for change in the partnership.

So, what is good listening? It's being actively engaged with the other person, whoever they are or whatever state they are in. It's listening attentively, showing you want to make contact with the person they really are. You do this by responding to what they actually say, not what you hope or imagine they've said. It's asking them to explain and say more if you don't understand, and knowing that you are willing and able to hear them. "Tell me..." is a great encourager.

Ask questions to show you want to know more, and particularly how they feel. Do for them what you would like done for you.

And listen to your own words as you speak. Do you come over as the person you really are or would like to be?

DIALOGUE

the first thing you say
the way that you say it
what you keep saying

      the way that you listen
      what you don't hear
      what makes you stop listening

what you don't say
the way you can't say it
the last thing you say

      what you can't cope with
      the way you're resistant
      that makes you not hear

Now we're ready to listen, shall we talk?

EMPATHY

My first job was in teaching, and from those years I discovered that I was drawn to children who found learning or life difficult. I felt intuitively that I needed to train to work with people in trouble, and a voice in my head said: "Be a marital counsellor". You should always listen to your intuition, because it takes you where you're meant to be. It connects you with a source inside you that isn't governed by logic, but is about what feels right. It expands your perspective and leads you to trust your own judgments, frees you up.

So, I start marital counselling. I love the work, and love the communication at a level of real trust with clients and making a relationship with them. I find I'm able to be where they are, and seem to connect with what they say. Connections are everywhere, if you think about it. The way we talk, the way we listen and hear what is being said; the way we respond and how much we give to each other.

Empathy is the ultimate connection, feeling *with*

another person, climbing into their shoes and connecting with their situation. Really listening takes you right into the heart of what someone is saying and feeling, so that you feel it too. I was wondering at first how I could work with clients without having always experienced the same situation myself. But when you realise it's about humanity, that we're all deeply linked one to another in our common goals, hopes and struggles, we are able to share anything and understand.

I recall one lady, Tricia, coming to see me, whose young adult child from her first marriage had suddenly been killed in an accident. This was threatening her stability and state of mind, and in turn was affecting her second marriage. Tricia had begun: "I don't know if you've ever lost a child who was number one in your life..." Clients often fear that the counsellor won't be able to understand their particular situation and the feeling they bring.

However, I just needed to look for the threads inside me that connected me to what she was saying and feeling. In Tricia's case, it was most of all about loss. I hadn't lost a child myself, but knew a lot about loss: family deaths, separation, loss of security and stability. Loss is such a big player in all our lives, because change inevitably brings loss in one way or another. Tricia spoke of other feelings: anger, pain, depression and grief. Human pain and suffering are easy to connect with if you just open your heart and listen.

We can also get closer to people if we show them that we can be weak too, that we don't always have to appear to be the strong ones. We don't always need to be on the listening end, we can tell our story too. Vulnerability and empathy are great connectors when we allow people to reach out to us to give us love and compassion. We don't need to be ashamed of our fragile side and lock it away.

The odd thing is that we grow up noticing and even looking for the differences in people, when we're all really just the same. It's not hard to share ups and downs with those around us, to listen, to hear or to tell our own story. If we do, that's connecting.

BRANCHING OUT

I remember on one of my early visits to Sebastian that he talked to me about energy. "Imagination and enthusiasm spark emotion and that's the fuel to take you to where you want to be. Imagination has no limits or boundaries."

I'd discovered that feeling, writing poetry for my creative writing group, when you can go inside your mind and see what's there today. You can find the mood, the words that feel and look right and, like painting, climb into them and be anywhere. Imagination can be exhilarating, and helps you to feel energy. "Inherently you know who you are and what direction you want to grow," he said. "Just grow and do what you want with it."

You can't help feeling different when you discover or give yourself this freedom for the first time. You find yourself able to have a go at new things, perhaps even discover a part of yourself you didn't know was there: maybe a forgotten skill or something you've always wanted to try. I believe imagination, coupled with risk-taking, allows you to branch out into the world as yourself, and to connect with other people. You feel part of the bigger picture and have the opportunity to make wider relationships and connections.

There's nothing so exciting and uplifting as coming across this sense of community energy and creativity. I went to visit Ely Cathedral one Saturday afternoon in October, and it was Harvest Festival the following day. The sunshine was filtering through the beautiful stained glass windows. We entered through the west door, expecting silence and peace, but instead walked into what felt like a busy market. The stillness had been replaced by a different sort of energy. That day there was an audible buzz of activity, friendly people coming forward to welcome us.

"Come and see what Harvest is all about." Diversity, growth and plenty laid out before us: a large tank of slithering eels, a glass-fronted beehive and bees hard at work in the honeycomb, piglets in a pen, a hen coop and a handful of hens busily rushing about behind the wire netting. There were tables laden with colourful local produce, red and green apples, root vegetables, jams and preserves, eggs and honey. Local primary schools had transformed aubergines and potatoes, carrots and turnips into all kinds of amazing birds and animals, frogs and hedgehogs sitting among whiskered cats and owls made from twigs and leaves. Posters and paintings too. Such creativity. The whole cathedral was alive. A living market-place, the sense of purpose and community quite remarkable.

We left the Cathedral marvelling at the spirit and energy we had felt. It was as if the community had laid before us all it had to show: the working together, the common belief, the desire to continue the tradition of autumn gratitude, in a place where people have come to worship over hundreds of years.

Have you found imagination and energy to help you branch out?

SAYING SORRY

To be a victim of crime is very upsetting, not just at the time, but the psychological after-effects may stay with you much longer. You can lose trust in your own sense of personal safety, and you may be left with recurring questions: Why me? Did they know me? Will they be back? Will I ever be able to forget?

A young boy, Darren, about fifteen years old had stolen an old car, parked in front of a house on his estate, gone joy-riding, and while showing off and driving too fast had crashed and written the car off. As a result he was referred to the Youth Offending Team, where I came across him while working as a volunteer.

Part of my role was to visit the victims of youth crime, and help support them in coming to terms with what had happened. Sometimes I would help them write a statement about how the offence had affected them, to use in work with the offender, or, if appropriate, special panel meetings could be arranged for victims and offenders to meet, should they both agree. That gives a chance for questions to be asked and answered about why, where and how the offence was committed. Hopefully this will bring some kind of resolution for the victim, and the offender will understand the impact of their offence. It's also an opportunity for the offender to apologise.

The young woman whose car had been damaged was keen to meet the boy, and he agreed. Both knew what the meeting was for, and the meeting was carefully prepared in advance. It's called Restorative Justice, and can be very powerful. The boy spoke first, very scared to meet his victim face to face, and began to explain the details of what he had done. Then it was her turn.

She started by asking him for the answers she needed. Then she told him what had upset her most. "It wasn't so much losing the car, though I've had to go to work by bus and really need a car for all kinds of reasons, but my father had given me his car only a month or so before he died. Just sitting in his car or driving around in it gave me time to think about him. All his maps and things were still in the car, and I felt very close to him. I've lost all that now."

You watch an offender while the victim speaks and you hold your breath. You wait to see how the offender will react. Sometimes very little. Other times a glimmer of understanding of the suffering the offence has caused. But with Darren, you could actually watch the impact on his face and feel his remorse, as the wider implications of wrecking her car dawned on him. You just knew that he would think twice the next time he started to get into trouble.

It's good for a victim to get a written apology, but better still if they get one face to face, like she got from Darren. That's when saying sorry can be an act of healing on both sides. You never know in these meetings what is going to hit home and awaken someone's conscience or provoke a heartfelt apology and desire to make amends, as happened that evening.

Let's not forget the hidden power of what we say, and how we say it. Particularly when we're saying sorry.

FORGIVENESS

"People make a habit out of not forgiving," Sebastian said to me. "Emotion is energy in motion. If you stop moving it gets stuck. You then hold all the bad stuff and punish yourself inadvertently." He added that holding the bad stuff is a way of trying to hang on to what's happened, so you don't do it again. "Don't go down this road. You need to get your feelings out in a better way."

There are times when we could forgive, but choose not to, waiting until much later to finally resolve things. But why would we do that? It would be much easier to resolve things in the present and move on. Except we tend not to. We hold on to unresolved issues and hurts, and battle with the bad feelings we're left with: 'poor me' / 'why should I forgive, it was their fault' / 'I know I'm to blame. I feel so bad I can't forgive myself.' Or even 'I want to punish them for how nasty they've been.'

Think of all those negative feelings we drag round with us. Probably the person you're really punishing is yourself. If we could get rid of guilt and blame how much easier life would be. "Forgive yourself quickly, and others just as quickly," Sebastian said to me. "Choose to forgive yourself easily, and choose that in place of fear."

That's it. Do it, let go and move on. Finding the choice inside yourself to forgive releases misery and resentment, and then you can be more content and at peace, both with yourself and others. After all, we all struggle with the same human emotions and dilemmas. Learning to be more forgiving to yourself leads you to forgiving others more easily.

We all just want to love and be loved. We're all the same, and knowing we're the same helps us to reach out to each other and understand better our linked human vulnerability and weakness. And helps us to forgive too.

JOY

It's funny the things that make me joyful. I was telling some friends the other day how I'd asked for some very strange things for my tenth birthday. "What would you like?" my parents had asked, and I remember excitedly telling them I wanted a lilac tree, a big roll of sellotape and a hot water bottle in the shape of a cat. They were the most special presents I had ever had and I can see myself opening them. I think it was the first time I'd felt the freedom of being different. The lilac tree even came with us when we moved house, such was its importance to me. Joy travels.

When I was young I think it was too easy for me to see life as a bit serious and about doing 'my best'. In so doing I forgot I was important too, and that's when you can lose the joy of feeling able to make choices for oneself. I recall Sebastian saying to me one day: "Lead your life how you want to lead it. A lot of times we lead life for other people, and when we get to the destination we realise we didn't want to get there. Then it's too late to recoup the time."

I knew immediately what he was talking about. It's when you get boxed in and agree to doing something when you don't really want to, which doesn't feel right and which you do just to please someone, but certainly not yourself. It's frightening how many people start out in careers according to someone else's wishes, expectations or demands. There's nothing worse than wishing you hadn't wasted part of your life doing something you never wanted to. Sebastian was the one who made me look at this. "Tell me what you like to do," he said one day. People don't often ask what you want or like. "Well," I said, "I like to write and paint, do the garden and make pictures," and added, "though I don't know how to do it."

"Change your thought to 'I do know what to do', because that opens up your intuition and allows the creativity to flow through," Sebastian said. "Say 'This is easy.'" When I got home I went back to a lovely book I'd been given, a creative art book 'Journal Spilling', about making art and writing come together in a spontaneous way; where you just write and paint or use any kind of technique and material. It had sounded a bit like being two or three again, sticking in torn scraps of paper, with no concern for straight edges, the aim being fun and freedom, mess rather than getting it perfect. Do it just for the fun of expressing yourself, without any rubbing out, painting over, any self-judgement. I'd been meaning to have a go, but hadn't dared until now. That's what Sebastian does. He gives me confidence just to be.

And it was *such* fun, letting my imagination run riot and not even knowing what would happen. I cut out words I'd typed in different fonts, flowers from a large piece of William Morris fabric I'd never used, and stuck them on a watercolour background of blues and yellows. There were places where the two colours merged to green, and onto this I put bright coloured birds, trees and fish cut from a Japanese calendar I'd kept. As I laid the colours and shapes down I started to feel excited and the 'not minding what happened' made me feel free and joyful. I think it was one of the first times I didn't mind what anyone thought of it, because it was my picture, and I liked it. Being spontaneous puts you in touch with the free and creative part of yourself, and being yourself is where real choices - and joy - begin.

I think we spend too much time weighed down by worries and anxiety. Bookshops are full of self-help books on every trouble known to man; television, websites, newspapers and magazines debate problems and miseries. But we tend not to read about joy in the same way. News can be depressing when the main angle is so negative.

So I thought I'd make a list of some of the things that made and make me joyful. I could have written many more things, but here are some, in no particular order:

- ❖ Having the incredible good fortune to find a partner to be loved by and love all my life.

- ❖ Having two amazing daughters.

- ❖ The garden, flowers and trees, and creating beauty and colour.

- ❖ Books, writing and words.

- ❖ Having our lovely family and grandchildren and the prospect of us all being reunited very soon after a long time abroad.

- ❖ Wonderful friends over many years.

- ❖ The joy of knowing, not just believing and trusting in God.

- ❖ Finding people to help me and teach me throughout my adult life, physically, emotionally and spiritually.

❖ Having had a stable and loving upbringing, with my very special sister, supported by parents who gave us boundaries and stability, vision and encouragement.

❖ The opportunities I have had to enjoy experiences, travel, meet so many people and learn from them.

❖ The joy of recovering twice from illness and burn out and coming back stronger.

❖ Having many years with Rosie, a quite irreplaceable dog.

❖ The safety and comfort of our home.

❖ Starting my own counselling partnership practice and it working so well.

❖ The opportunities to grow and develop all the time and not stand still.

❖ Oh yes, and the day my younger daughter got married:

MAY MORNING

And some time, make the time
to sit in a room
filled with early morning,
slanted sunlight through cool glass,
like the day they married
and the stillness and beauty
of nothing and everything
was caught in the throat of a day
only just waking up.

Not a sound anywhere, not that day,
when trusses of pale lilac and bluebells
were holding their breath,
and you just had to close your eyes
and remember each blade of grass,
how the clouds moved,
the exact shade of the pink azalea,
everything right.

CHANGE

I used to work a lot with helping people to change. That's really a big part of what marital counselling is about. I used to say to clients when they came to see me: "I haven't got any solutions, so I'm not going to give you any advice. But what I do offer you is to climb into whatever problem or crisis you're bringing to me and help you with the muddle and the stress, and particularly all your feelings about it. We'll work together to understand how you've come to this point, and then I'll help you work out what you want to change about your situation. We'll set up a strategy together for making those changes, and I'll support you while you try to put them into practice."

Marriage and relationships are a tricky area, because in an intimate relationship we are still individuals. His views may be very different from hers. What's 'the right way' to do things, how to manage money, sex, children, what toothpaste to have. What feels like a generous concession in the beginning (because you want to please) can end up as an irritation and a cause for argument, even a power struggle. But although not necessarily the same needs and wants, their differing perceptions are equally valid. Two people look out of the same window and don't see the same things. As Sebastian says: "No-one else can see what you see, because they're not you."

Another thing is that we are changing all the time. Everything is changing all around us: day and night, the months, the seasons, the years, and along with that we get older every day. Our circumstances change: good or less good health, more or less money, more or less responsibility for growing family, ageing parents. Differing demands at each life stage, which require us to be flexible and adapt to the new challenges which we will inevitably meet. Scary sometimes and often needing new skills which we haven't learnt before.

But it's what brings interest and excitement too, like going on holiday to somewhere you haven't been before. Everywhere looks new and that can be very stimulating, but you may be one of the people that like to go to the same place every year. That can be a stabilising point for you, if your life is very stressful and demanding at home. That's the point really. Change is stressful in itself, and we have to choose how to manage it, or if we are fearful about what is ahead, avoid it. "People have to decide themselves that they want to change and move forward," says Sebastian.

So what makes the desire to change turn into a tangible step forward? I wondered about how I'd managed to change so much since I'd been ill:

1. I'd accepted the situation that I was in and its implications.

2. I'd not been afraid to ask for help and ask for support for a while.

3. I'd been determined to get well, and to learn strategies for my recovery.

4. I looked back to what I knew already that, when I had faced difficult times before, I had come through safely. This was another step on my 'ladder' that I was meant to take.

5. I saw the rest time as an opportunity to read and study to advance during this transition.

6. I wrote down what I was told when I went to see Sebastian, and kept re-reading it and trying to incorporate it inside me.

7. I tried to put into practice what resonated with me and felt right.

8. I was lucky that I believed in and had total trust in Sebastian and liked him to challenge my old unhelpful habits.

9. I felt desperate some days to leave all the bad parts of my life behind, and that motivated me towards change.

10. Also I felt there were lots of things I wanted to do, like writing, now my energy was back.

Recently I've been reading the Dalai Lama's book 'The Art of Happiness', and have been noticing how he sees the 'process of change.' In his chapter on change he lists the various steps:

- Learning
- Developing conviction of the need to change
- Determination
- Effort and enthusiasm, what he calls 'urgency' to solve problems.

I could see from that, that I had been on the right track, but his writing makes me aware how shallow my patience is and how his calm serenity allows him a lifetime of slow learning and tolerance and compassion and faith. But I am changing, and that's good.

ANGELS

On one of my early visits to Sebastian I picked up a leaflet about his healing work, which talked about energy flowing through the meridians or pathways of your body, interlinking mind, body and spirit. He calls energy the train, and your meridians the tracks it runs on. His job is to find blockages on the line and move energy through them, so that the body repairs itself and heals. But beyond that he works with divine energy to channel healing and guidance through himself to those he works with.

I'd read many books about energy, and Chris, my homeopath and acupuncturist, who has looked after me for years, had always talked about *qi* or *ch'i*, the basic life-force in the body. I'd built up through him a belief in the power of the body to heal itself, but you need to see energy as not only inside yourself, but around you too, and be aware if that energy gets stuck, either by some imbalance or by some emotional disturbance, we may start to become unwell.

We have a soul as well as a body, by which I mean a

divine spark of energy that connects us to God. We talk about 'mind, body and soul' and finding a 'soul mate', or listening to 'soul music', but if we aren't actively aware of and draw from this spark we may ignore its potential to bring different values and a different sort of energy and creativity into our lives.

Sebastian talked about the different levels of divine energy. "You have a guardian angel who calls on others to help. This angel has been with you since before you came to this earth and will be with you all the time, and with you when you die." I didn't know what to say. This is something else. "Your angel is of a different vibration and is just light and energy." He explained that there is a higher level of divine energy which he is able to connect with in order to channel, and for him this is Archangel Michael and the angelic realm. This is beyond my understanding.

He talked about the importance of expanding one's vision and not limiting what we see or think by fixing ideas and being unwilling to embrace change. That's one of the things I love about Sebastian. He's always challenging me to look at things in a new expanding way.

So I have a guardian angel. Did I know that before? Well, yes and no. There had been many times during my recovery years when I had experienced and read about things I couldn't explain in logical terms. Times when I had been helped in my work to understand and interpret: a direction which didn't feel directly from me. I had noticed connections between happenings, and was aware of synchronicity around me: that is perceiving connections and making some kind of personal interpretation from them often leading to something significant. I had had dreams which felt important too.

But actual angels? Our family didn't do angels. I'd been brought up within the confines of church doctrine and I don't remember angels coming into it, except in hymns and Bible readings, especially at Christmas. And I loved the way religious art depicted archangels and angels in churches and galleries: holy, halo-bearing, winged attendants of God, or divine messengers, angels in many diverse roles, glorifying, protecting, consoling and celebrating. So for me angels, I think, were for painters, and people I read about that felt they had always had guardian angels to watch over them, and who had looked upon them as an integral part of themselves since childhood.

I pondered this reaction of mine to hearing I, too, had a guardian angel:

❖ Do I believe in their unseen presence on this earthly plane? I suppose my answer has to be, yes. I have understood enough to realise what I know is infinitesimal and limited by my imagination and old fixed beliefs. Therefore I am willing to expand my mind and soul to believe in the possibility.

❖ Angels are not of this world, because they bridge Heaven & Earth, and possess energy of a different frequency from us. We are all made of energy, but our energy cannot compare with that of the angels, because they are not confined by our restraints of time and place, and are filled with Divine energy. This pure spirit of love allows them to be with anyone, anywhere, at all times.

❖ Do I feel worthy of having a guardian angel? I would have loved to consider the possibility, as a child. It's such a comforting picture, the idea of protection and guidance and never being alone, but I never really dared to consider it. However I am in a totally different place now, in all senses.

❖ Angels are full of light and love and bring us support in what we do, as well as giving healing and comfort. I found a poem I'd written many years ago, which ended with the line: 'angels watching over us.' Had I believed in angels all along?

❖ I do have this awareness that I am protected and led somehow, that beyond the ordinary self there is a higher self. I believe the more you are open to that possibility, the more good energy and creativity will come to you, which you can pass back into the world.

Sebastian says: "Whether people believe in God or not, God, Archangels & angels are there. What they believe, if they don't believe in them, is of no consequence. God, Archangels & angels are always there and love them."

THE WAY I SEE IT

The way I see it is

we have grown stronger
adversity turning us to face each other
turning us back strengthened
so that together and apart
we have looked out
seen rainbows and walked along colours
of red, orange and indigo
to where our gold lies.

The way I see it is

we have always loved each other
finding not what we had expected
nor even the dreams of early years
but things so amazing
so incredible that if we die tomorrow
we shall have had fireworks and Albertine roses
soaring eagles and the still smooth waters
of a calm-day lake
angels watching over us.

FINDING ANGELS

I'm sort of a 'don't know' where angels are concerned, interested, but rather frightened to nail my colours to the mast. It's 2008 and I'm taking time out to recover from overwork. I turn to gentle music and reflective books. I remember reading a newspaper review of a book: 'Angels in my Hair', Lorna Byrne telling the story of her life in rural Ireland and how she grew up believing in and seeing angels. From this she had developed spiritual insight and worked with people to help them with their problems. I decided to read it. Part of me felt uncomfortable choosing a book like that. This was definitely not what I would normally read and certainly not a book I would easily discuss in conversation. But I was somehow drawn to read it.

The book shocked me with its open honesty and simplicity of faith, this young woman accepting the presence of angels around her from her earliest days, and trusting them in all her contact with them. She made it all sound so normal and acceptable that angels were visible to her and just part of her life. This left me slightly disconcerted, but wondering too. If she sees angels, how many other people do and don't talk about it?

Working with Fenella, I found that my therapy was changing as we talked more about spirituality. She started a small meditation group and I joined. I was starting to move among people who talked easily about things like angels and chakras, energy and grounding. What had felt odd and slightly embarrassing at first now became more normal. My world was expanding again.

I found that as I began to embrace the possibilities of things I'd never considered before, the more they were likely to actually happen. I found connections between things I read and things that I came across. It was like seeing the world through new glasses, so that on walks in the country or driving around I felt I noticed more and was more aware of what I saw and I felt happier too.

We decided to spend a week in Cornwall in the spring, staying a night with friends in Somerset en route. On day two as we were driving into Devon, I discovered my bunch of house keys (including alarm de-activator) and car key were missing. I rang our friends, who scoured their house for them, to no avail. There was nothing to do, except hope that they would magically turn up in the case or car, a pocket, a bag- any of the places we had searched repeatedly. But they didn't.

One week later we drove home, and as we turned into the drive, beside my car, close to the road and highly visible, was my bunch of keys, lying on the stones. The house was as we had left it, my car too. No break-in using the house and alarm keys. No convenient removal of our belongings in my car. How did no-one see the keys? They'd lain in the middle of the drive fully exposed for *one week*. It felt like a miracle. Were the angels looking after our house? For the first time I believed they had protected us.

I found that Fenella's spiritual workshops gave me another forum to meet and discuss with like-minded people. You learn a lot talking to others in the same place of exploration as you. For some time I'd wondered about a weird experience I'd had one Sunday morning a year before. We'd been in bed and looked out of the window to see a few white feathers dropping from the sky. We knew there were pigeons nesting in the big pine tree in the garden, but the feathers were nowhere near the tree. Where were they coming from? We got up and went outside and looked up to the chimney where the pigeons used to sit sometimes. Nothing. No birds in the tree, no birds on the roof, no birds to be seen, *anywhere*. And for about ten minutes white feathers continued to fall from the sky, like snowflakes in a gentle snowstorm, settling on the grass and speckling it white. We looked next door on both sides. Not a white feather to be seen. Just in our garden. Neither of us understood where they came from.

At a workshop some time later someone talked about angels and white feathers and the memory of the strange happening in the garden that Sunday morning came back. When I got home I looked up white feathers on Google. 'White feathers are a common angel sign', it said. Nowadays it doesn't seem so impossible.

Nor did it seem as frightening when I had a very bad fall, tripping and being pitched forward onto the back of an oak chair, my nose and forehead taking the full brunt of it. I recall despite being badly hurt thinking instantly: 'This is going to be okay. I know I will recover, because I am not alone. I know I am blessed, because I am still able to think and speak, so my brain isn't damaged.' That feeling stayed with me constantly over the months that followed. It was a sense of knowing and understanding that I had never had before, that this accident was just something to deal with and that I would be helped to do so.

It makes a lot of difference when you don't feel alone inside.

STILLNESS AND LIGHT

One of the lines from the Dalai Lama's book 'The Art of Happiness' has stuck in my mind. He says: "True spirituality is a mental attitude that you can practise at any time." I'd been trying to get my thoughts together on stillness and meditation when I remembered this line from his book. He's the fourteenth Tibetan Buddhist High Lama and lives now in Northern India in exile. He writes books, teaches and lectures, promoting peace and happiness all over the world.

What I find amazing about him is the accessibility of his words, how he can bring his wisdom down to the everyday practical needs of ordinary people and conveys simply what we can do to manage our daily struggles. He says that we shouldn't see spirituality as something just to do with rituals and practice, but see our everyday behaviour coloured by what we have learned and learn every day. This is where I come back to stillness and meditation.

More people are into meditation these days, finding that they need some place to escape to, in order to slow down and find some peace. The world is so rushed and pressured that the human mind can be easily overwhelmed. The rewards from meditation can be huge, because mind, body and soul are interlinked, so all benefit from it, especially the body, which becomes grounded and centred, less stressed and with more energy.

In 2006, Chris, an expert in many alternative medicine techniques and a spiritual healer too, felt meditation would help my stress. He invited me to an introductory session he was running, and began by explaining that meditation could be both the way to calm the mind and at a higher level a search for unity with God.

He used the analogy of a spinning disc to describe our stress-filled lives. Most of us spin wildly round the edge of the disc, and our aim is to reach the middle point, which is the static point of stillness. From there we can start to reach out to anywhere on the disc. I think that analogy of the disc works well, because we hurtle through our days and are at risk of getting thrown by the momentum. Most of us don't realise this of course, until we get ill or crumble under the weight of all we put ourselves through.

So, we are seeking peace in the silence and will try to do this by finding the still point inside ourselves. We want to learn how to let go of our incessant preoccupation with things outside us. There's always something to think about and the human mind never settles. Where do you begin, and is it possible to stop thinking, even for a few seconds? It isn't easy at first, but by just relaxing and concentrating on the sound of your breathing in the silence you can divert attention away from your thoughts.

Choose a quiet comfortable place. Sit, close your eyes and shut out the world. Start to listen to the rhythm of your breathing in and out, and feel the flow of it through your body. At first, thoughts will keep coming into your mind, but you don't need to listen to them. You can let them float away, like clouds, and allow yourself to come back to them later. Just keep your attention on your breathing and feel relaxed.

I found it really hard to stop my mind wandering at first, but I knew it didn't matter. You need to be kind to yourself and say "I can't get it wrong". As you practise it gets easier. I remember the first time I managed not to think for a minute or so, and it felt amazingly peaceful and calm.

I have a particular place at home where I always meditate, so just sitting there feels special. I have a small candle which I always light, which for me is about calling light down into my meditation. I used to forget to do my meditation sometimes in the early days, but gradually it became more important to me, and now it's become an absolute priority every day and I draw great strength from it.

It's also a place I can be myself, just as I am. At first I used to think: "I can't meditate today, because I'm in a bad mood, or really worried about something. I won't be able to sit still and not think about all this stuff going on in my mind." Actually that's a very good time to choose to meditate, because it takes away or eases the feelings. Whatever's going on is helped by meditation and allows you to be more aware, so that solutions often seem to emerge in the calm and silence.

Sebastian says: "Meditate for as long as you want, when and because you want to. It's not about being in control. It's about being present and still." Meditation is about moving beyond the usual restlessness of thought and body to find some new level of peace and awareness. It's about being present in the now and can be about finding our spiritual self.

Meditation can operate at so many different levels, depending on what we want from it: a way to find calmness and stillness in a busy life, or maybe develop it into a more spiritual time, when we look inside ourselves in a search for closeness with God.

ENDINGS

I don't think we give much time to the idea of endings. We seem to live in a world so fast moving that when we finish one thing we just go on to the next. We're used to commodities like kettles and washers breaking down and we expect to just go out and buy another. It's very much a throw-away society. I remember as a child our freezing cold scullery, green paint and a frosted window. By the deep white sink hung a little wire basket on a wire handle, and in the basket were tail-end bits of soap which frothed in the water when you shook it. Nothing wasted back then. We hung on to things in those days.

But I'm really talking about significant 'endings', like the end of a relationship either by inevitability or choice. Like when you lose someone very dear to you, a partner, member of the family, special friend, anyone you love. You can feel that hollow sense of loss afterwards. I remember the day the phone rang and being told my mother had been rushed into hospital and probably wouldn't recover. To realise that I was driving to see her for the last time threw me into a turmoil of emotions: fear and panic, especially that I would arrive too late, anger at the red traffic lights and traffic that didn't seem to understand they needed to move aside to let me through, and a heavy, mounting sense of an approaching finality.

I remember too, us all sitting with her at her bedside and thinking we must all have time alone with her, to make our special endings with her; time to say our own goodbyes in the way we all needed. Some endings leave huge memories, and you want to end up with memories of resolution and peace. I find my memories of that day still comfort me a lot, and certainly did in the early days without her. Sadness is different from regretting something you didn't say or do. Endings often really are final and then you don't get a second chance.

Endings are part of life for all of us, and yet even the ones you plan for, like moving house and leaving familiar faces and places behind can be stressful. Or going to a new place of work or school. Change is always demanding: goodbyes, as well as the newness of what lies ahead. We may face personal loss of some kind: perhaps the gradual ending of good health, good eyesight, mobility, anything that changes and then limits or fails. Redundancy, losing your job, separation, so many situations can entail and require large amounts of stamina and courage to move on to change and build or adapt to something new.

Endings aren't easy and it's easy to ignore them. Or fudge them, particularly in ending relationships, such as using texts or announcing on Facebook that a relationship is over. It is because dealing with such painful and harsh realities is so difficult that many couples go for joint counselling, where it feels safer to express raw truths and volatile emotions. After all, an intimate relationship holds two people, and it can be scary to share reasons and explanations for the ending of loving years together. Separation can leave you facing the loss of part of yourself, the bit that you invested in that person. Endings do challenge our sense of safety and security and we need time to reframe and rebuild our sense of self.

I think I now look back on each 'ending' I've experienced as a point of growth, and realise I learned something new about myself each time. I believe it is this awareness that has given me strength to trust myself, pick myself up and deal with loss and change.

So what will help you deal with endings and manage them better? I thought about what I've learned so far:

❖ Endings are when something comes to its

completion, either at the end of its term or when circumstances change.

❖ The more sudden and unexpected they are, the more disconcerted you may feel by them. The more you expect an ending, the more time you have to prepare and get ready for what is going to happen, like retirement or possibly redundancy.

❖ Endings can demand much from us, because they inevitably involve change, and depending on our attitude to change, we can handle them calmly and with acceptance, or find ourselves overwhelmed.

❖ Not all endings bring negative outcomes or feelings. Some bring new opportunities and the opening of new doors. I remember Sebastian saying to me: "It's good to push your boundaries, and realise not everything has to be the same it's always been."

❖ Change is filled with the spirit of energy and newness, and as such, keeps life from getting stale. We can look at endings as negative, as in 'Why me?' and feel a sense of sadness, injustice or even anger, or we can try to ride whatever happens with some level of acceptance.

❖ Some endings bring escape from situations which have caused suffering or unhappiness, like an abusive relationship. Choosing to put oneself first and take oneself away from a situation which is causing you great distress, may be a new beginning for you, rather than an ending.

❖ Making the choice to end something yourself can be liberating, empowering and life-enhancing.

I know I used to be very fixed and liked things to turn out as I expected. I knew what I needed to happen for me to feel safe, and was unhappy when circumstances dictated otherwise. Gradually I learned you can't control the world around you and if you get to know yourself and what works for you, you can trust your instincts to get you through even the worst scenarios.

Be aware. Let things evolve and don't look too far ahead. Lean on your intuition. Does this feel right? If it does, do it. If it doesn't feel right, don't.

ACCEPTANCE

"Things just are." Three little words to change perspective on life. Eckhart Tolle in his book "A New Earth" tells the story of J. Krishnamurti, a renowned Indian spiritual teacher who gave talks all his life. At one of them he asked whether his audience wanted to know the secret of his contented and centred spiritual life. They waited expectantly for his answer. Back came the reply: "I don't mind what happens."

At first it sounds a very simple answer, but then when you think about it, it seems very hard to put into practice. How can you not mind what happens? How can you go through life just accepting what comes? What about the difficult times? And surely I must prepare for what lies ahead? I must have hope, or life becomes empty. Don't I need to take steps to make good things happen, certainly to avoid problems? So that suggests putting effort into making sure things will be as good as they can be for me, my family and community.

But what he's saying is 'not minding what happens'

opens up your heart to the possibility of anything happening, and that being just fine. That you *can* wake up in the morning and not need to control the outcome of things: today I will accept things as they are, both good and bad, seeing each to be closely linked to the other, and a fine line between them.

Sometimes an occasion we fear, or one that suddenly comes upon us out of the blue and upsets us, turns out to be a better experience than we expected, and the one we couldn't wait for leaves a memory of disappointment. I look back at what I see as the real suffering moments in my life and find in them meaning and depth. This turns them into something beyond a sad or bad memory, like when my mother was suddenly taken critically ill and we were given some hours to sit with her, before she passed away. It felt a blessing to be allowed to be there for her at the end of her life. That thought brings acceptance and peace.

Acceptance is made much easier if we don't fret and fuss about things, wanting them to be this or that, being disappointed if they aren't as we expect or hope. If we let things be, just as they are, we can stop trying to control them, and some things we can't control anyway.

Peace lies in not expecting, not labeling things and judging people and situations. Peace lies in accepting and dealing with things as they happen, and being flexible and strong enough not to have to fear that which lies ahead.

Do you mind what happens?

THOUGHTS FOR EVERY DAY

❖ Take things as they come.

❖ Allow mysteries in your life to unravel at their appropriate time.

❖ Live every day as if it were your last and plan as if you'll live forever.

❖ If you look on things as a burden that's what they become. Your body can only respond to what you think and tell it to do.

❖ We are all connected. You never know how far things reach. Throw a pebble into a pond, and the ripples go down very deep, as well as across.

❖ Be flexible like bamboo. It's hollow, which gives it flexibility and strength. If you're rigid a storm can break you.

❖ The only power anyone has over you is the power that you give them. And if you give it away, you can't blame anyone else.

❖ Remember that nobody sees and feels the exact same as you.

❖ Doing and Being are two separate things. Being is in your heart and Doing is in your head.

❖ Love is greater than fear.

BOOK LIST

These are just some of the books that inspired me, helped me to start learning, and opened my eyes in the beginning. They have all in some way taught me to look at the world and my part in it in a new way. I hope that they may do the same for you.

The Tibetan Art of Serenity, Christopher Hansard

The Tibetan Art of Positive Thinking, Christopher Hansard

The Power of Now, Eckhart Tolle

A New Earth, Eckhart Tolle

The Tibetan Book of Living and Dying, Sogyal Rinpoche

The Wheel of Life, Elizabeth Kübler-Ross

Finding Sanctuary, Abbot Christopher Jamison

Finding Happiness, Abbot Christopher Jamison

Tao Te Ching, Lao Tzu (Translated by Stephen Mitchell)

Change your Thoughts, Change your Life: Living the Wisdom of the Tao, Wayne W. Dyer

The Art of Happiness, HH Dalai Lama & Howard C. Cutler

The Book of Secrets, Deepak Chopra

Reinventing the Body, Resurrecting the Soul, Deepak Chopra

Buddha, Deepak Chopra

A Lightworker's Way, Doreen Virtue

Healing with Angels, Doreen Virtue

Angels in my Hair, Lorna Byrne

Comfortable with Uncertainty, Pema Chodron

Peace is Every Step: the Path of Mindfulness in everyday life, Thich Nhat Hahn

EPILOGUE

Three years ago I would never have imagined myself writing a book, but I hadn't met Sebastian then. I didn't realise that working with him would be so inspirational, and would lead to me wanting to write about our meetings. The energy that I take home from them stays with me and empowers me to move forward, stronger, calmer and wiser.

I want to end the book with my gratitude to the people who have supported me in the writing of this book. Special thanks to you, Howard and Helen, for your endless love, support and patience, and most of all for believing in me. Fenella, thank you for all your help, your loving encouragement and understanding of my vision.

Thank you, Sebastian, for your unconditional love and support, and for encouraging me early on to write down what you say. The wisdom you channel from above forms the backbone of my story, and I have reproduced in my book the exact words you pass on down to me. Without this, and you, there would have been no book.